BRITISH RAILWAYS

PAST and PRESENT

No 60

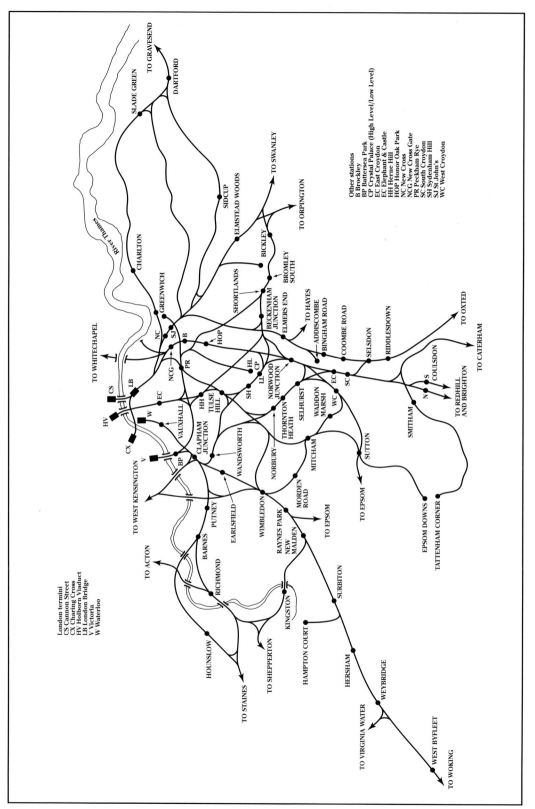

London termini
CS Cannon Street
CX Charing Cross
HV Holborn Viaduct
LB London Bridge
V Victoria
W Waterloo

Other stations
B Brockley
BP Battersea Park
CP Crystal Palace (High Level/Low Level)
EC East Croydon
EC Elephant & Castle
HH Herne Hill
HOP Honor Oak Park
NC New Cross
NCG New Cross Gate
PR Peckham Rye
SC South Croydon
SH Sydenham Hill
SJ St John's
WC West Croydon

TO GRAVESEND
SLADE GREEN
DARTFORD
TO SWANLEY
SIDCUP
ELMSTEAD WOODS
TO ORPINGTON
CHARLTON
BICKLEY
SHORTLANDS
BROMLEY SOUTH
GREENWICH
BECKENHAM JUNCTION
ELMERS END
TO HAYES
ADDISCOMBE
BINGHAM ROAD
COOMBE ROAD
SELSDON
RIDDLESDOWN
TO OXTED
NC
SJ
B
HOP
HL
CP
NCG
PR
HH
TULSE HILL
SH
NORWOOD JUNCTION
SELHURST
WADDON MARSH
WC
EC
SC
COULSDON
TO CATERHAM
River Thames
TO WHITECHAPEL
CS
LB
HV
EC
W
VAUXHALL
CX
V
BP
CLAPHAM JUNCTION
WANDSWORTH
THORNTON HEATH
NORBURY
MITCHAM
SUTTON
SMITHAM
N
S
TO REDHILL AND BRIGHTON
TO WEST KENSINGTON
TO ACTON
PUTNEY
BARNES
EARLSFIELD
WIMBLEDON
RAYNES PARK
NEW MALDEN
MORDEN ROAD
TO EPSOM
TO EPSOM
TO EPSOM
EPSOM DOWNS
TATTENHAM CORNER
RICHMOND
KINGSTON
SURBITON
TO SHEPPERTON
TO STAINES
HOUNSLOW
HAMPTON COURT
HERSHAM
WEYBRIDGE
TO VIRGINIA WATER
WEST BYFLEET
TO WOKING

A simplified map of the railways of South London covered by this book, showing locations featured or referred to in the text.

BRITISH RAILWAYS

PAST and PRESENT

No 60
South London Suburban Railways

Michael H. C. Baker

Past and Present

Past & Present Publishing Ltd

First published in 2009

British Library Cataloguing in Publication Data

A catalogue record for this book is available from the British Library.

ISBN 978 1 85895 262 8

Past & Present Publishing Ltd
The Trundle
Ringstead Road
Great Addington
Kettering
Northants NN14 4BW

Tel/Fax: 01536 330588
email: sales@nostalgiacollection.com
Website: www.nostalgiacollection.com

Printed and bound in the Czech Republic

GLOSSARY
of Electric Multiple Unit (EMU) classifications

(The number preceding each indicates the number of cars forming each set)

EPB Electro-Pneumatic Brakes
SUB Suburban
PEP Prototype high-density EMU
WES Wessex (Class 442)
REP Restaurant/buffet, Electro-Pneumatic brakes
TC   Trailer Car (sets)

JOP Juniper (Class 458)
COR Corridor
CIG Corridor (throughout, with) Interconnecting Gangway
PUL Pullman
PAN Pantry (car included)
BIG Buffet (car included, with) Interconnecting Gangway
NOP No lavatories, electro-pneumatic brakes
NOL No Lavatories

CONTENTS

CLAPHAM JUNCTION: In 1965 scruffy rebuilt Bulleid 'light Pacific' No 34104 *Bere Alston* and its crew take it easy in the carriage sidings.

This sign was erected in June 2005, official recognition having been given that not only is Clapham Junction the busiest station in the UK, some 2,000 trains passing through each weekday, but also on this reckoning that it is also the busiest in the whole of Europe. The number of passengers that pass through is increasing and approaching a staggering half a million each day – around 430,000 at the last count – although many of them do not actually alight. Of those that do, some 40% change trains. *Both MHCB*

BECKENHAM JUNCTION: On 30 December 1956 '01' Class 0-6-0 No 31048 brings into the station the stock of a special train organised to mark the centenary of the Mid Kent line between Lewisham and Beckenham Junction, opened on 1 January 1857, while a 2NOL EMU heads a train arriving from Victoria via Crystal Palace Low Level. The '01s', designed by Stirling, originated on the South Eastern Railway between 1878 and 1899, being rebuilt by Wainwright. No 31048 was one of the last survivors. It is hauling an LB&SCR-built push-and-pull unit. The 2NOLs were formed by the Southern Railway in the mid-1930s from converted LSWR steam stock.

In the summer of 2006 a Waterloo International to Paris Gare du Nord Eurostar approaches Beckenham Junction.

Finally, sneaking around the bend into Beckenham Junction in May 2008 is Croydon Tramlink car No 2536. With the first inauguration of Eurostar in 1994, then with Tramlink from 2000, this seemingly ordinary suburban station became one of the most interesting in the country. *R. C. Riley/MHCB (2)*

INTRODUCTION

One somewhat surprising aspect of putting together these pictures is the predominance of things arboreal in the story we have to tell. The replacement of multiple units, disappearance of steam engines and goods yards, rebuilding of stations and so forth were all anticipated, but I hadn't realised that trees would figure so prominently. In a world where we quite rightly agonise over the disappearance of rain forests, it is perhaps not realised that in a very tiny way the suburban railways of south London have, over the last 50 or so years, been doing their best to redress the balance. Returning to locations I hadn't visited for decades, I wondered where the railway had gone. Unaware of any abandonments – pretty well unknown in this part of the network anyhow – often all I could see were mini-hayfields, jungle-like bushes or full-scale forests, or so it seemed. Bromley was a case in point. Back in the 1970s the top floor of a multi-storey car park afforded an excellent, unobstructed view of trains approaching Bromley South station from the north. Returning on a wet October morning in 2008 I was confronted by the most glorious autumnal display of golds and rich, deep yellows, extending to the height of the car park, with, far below, odd glimpses of trains seemingly burrowing their way through this cornucopia of foliage. No doubt this has something to do with complaints of 'leaves on the line', although in truth we get through most autumns without any great problems.

We love to moan about the railways, especially if we use them to commute, and those of the south London suburbs have always come in for their fair – perhaps, more accurately, unfair – share of complaints. That once very popular TV series, *The Fall and Rise of Reginald Perrin*, encapsulated the life of a commuter in the south-west suburbs. Each morning the hero, played originally by the late and much-missed Leonard Rossiter, never managed to arrive on time in his office, which although supposed to be in central London looked exactly like the sort of between-the-wars factory estate one would have found in Surbiton, New Malden or some such location. His opening line to his intermittently lusted-after secretary would always be 'points failure at Wimbledon', 'floods at Hampton Court', 'dog on the line at Vauxhall', or some such comment.

Commuting has never been much fun, although the old compartment-type EMUs, whether the wooden-bodied variety, which the never spendthrift Southern Railway inherited, or the steel Bulleid ones, were worse than anything around today. There was a time when I used them regularly – indeed, when I was growing up they were my norm – but after several years far away from the Southern, I boarded one of the last compartment carriages running in an EPB set at East Croydon and, sitting with my knees in very close proximity to a total stranger sitting opposite, was appalled by the experience. The effect in the cramped, packed compartment was nothing short of claustrophobic, while the riding qualities, once thought perfectly acceptable, were something to be endured.

The first Bulleid EMUs of 1941 were known as the 'Queen of Shebas' on account of being 'very great trains', but 'great' only applied to their seating capacity, which for a four-coach unit was a staggering 456, made possible by their concave-shaped sides, a feature that persisted on both new suburban and, perhaps surprisingly, main-line stock into British Railways days. Such was the demand – and such is the demand today – that it has to be thus, with as many passengers crammed into a train and as many trains crammed on to the track as is humanly possible, bearing in mind safety requirements.

Given the complexity of the network and the frequency of the trains using it, the suburban lines south of the Thames have an excellent safety record. However, there have been serious accidents. The first I can recall was between South Croydon and Purley Oaks on a foggy

October morning in 1947. Some of my 2B classmates at Whitgift Middle School were travelling in the rear carriages of the 8.04am from Tattenham Corner, which crashed into the 7.33am from Haywards Heath. Although shaken, they were unhurt, but 32 people were killed and 58 injured. They got down on to the track and had to pass the front of their train and the rear of the other, being confronted by scenes that, understandably, upset them deeply and about which they refused to talk.

Even worse was the St Johns accident of 4 December, 1957. Again fog was the key element in the disaster. Ninety people died and 175 were injured when the 4.56pm Cannon Street to Ramsgate steam train ran into the back of the 5.18pm Charing Cross to Hayes electric train, the derailed locomotive, a Bulleid 'Pacific', bringing down an overbridge. A Holborn Viaduct to Dartford electric train, approaching the bridge, just managed to stop in time. I was hitchhiking home to Thornton Heath from RAF West Malling that evening, and at about the time of the collision was in a lorry approaching Sidcup, some 5 miles distant. At one point so thick was the fog that I had to get out of the cab and guide the driver around a roundabout and on to his exit road.

The nearest I ever got, or ever hope to get, to a serious accident was on a visit to Clapham Junction around 1950. I was ensconced at the trainspotters' favourite venue, the Waterloo end of the up Western Section main-line platform, and was idly watching a porter on the opposite platform pushing a four-wheel barrow loaded with milk churns. Suddenly one of the front wheels twisted, shopping-trolley-wise, towards and over the platform edge. The porter yelled and tried to hang on but trolley and churns tipped on to the track. I heard a high-pitched electric whistle and whirled round to see one of the Southern Railway-built 1925-vintage EMUs, not scheduled to stop at Clapham Junction and therefore travelling at around 40mph, heading straight for the wreckage only yards away, the motorman standing at his controls, an expression of horror on his face. Over the years there have been several accidents where such a trolley has derailed a train, with fatal results to passengers and those waiting on the platform. This time the Gods smiled down on Clapham Junction. Maybe the speed of the train, combined with its heavy motor bogie, gave it sufficient impetus, but it ploughed through the wreckage, sending a shower of milk over the track and platforms. There was a cloud of brown smoke and the train rocked, but held the rails and came to a halt partly out of the station. One of the number-spotting fraternity later insisted that he had seen a lady coming out of a phone box on the platform at the very moment of impact, who had been covered from head to foot in milk, but this claim was viewed, rightly I think, with deep suspicion. The event was dramatic enough without need of embellishment. In what would today have seemed a remarkably short time, the train moved out, the track was cleared and within half an hour things were back to normal.

In many ways attitudes were more relaxed back then, not always for the best; young trainspotters and enthusiasts took risks that, looking back, were somewhat foolhardy. Some of the original locations are impossible to repeat exactly today because I either stood on or right beside the track. I very seldom did this where there was a third rail, but it was not unknown. I did not have permission and any railwaymen who saw me turned a blind eye. Try that today and you'd be lucky to get away with 50 years in the Tower of London!

On more than one occasion in the last two or three years, despite being armed with the British Transport Police's letter regarding photography on stations, I have been told on some pretty minor suburban stations that 'photography is not allowed' and to put my camera away. This even happened at my original home station, Thornton Heath. On the one hand I was quite pleased to think that what I had until then considered a pretty unremarkable suburban backwater was now of great strategic importance. On the other, I thought could there be anything more stupid than an edict issued to staff that all persons, even elderly white-haired gentlemen, seen using a camera are terrorist suspects. This, regardless of the fact that at another of my locals, East Croydon, at any time of the day or night dozens of passengers are using mobile phones, all of which are capable of taking photographs, that at the main-line termini people are always taking pictures of friends and relations arriving and departing, and that, above all, at the wonderfully refurbished St Pancras, terminus of Eurostar, and surely a potential terrorist target if ever there was one, it is almost impossible to hear the sound of croissants and bottles of champagne being loaded for the clicking of cameras by all and sundry.

However, having got that off my chest, it cannot be denied that rail travel around the south London suburbs, despite a few black spots, has got a good deal better over the years. The units designed for suburban travel are a good deal more comfortable than they used to be. Automatic doors makes journeys safer – and, in winter, warmer. The clear demarcation

SYDENHAM HILL is set in a cutting below the hill on which the Crystal Palace stood from 1853 to 1936 and which gave its name to the district. 'King Arthur' 4-6-0 No 769 *Sir Balin*, seen shortly after delivery from Glasgow and before being fitted with smoke deflectors, has charge of the all-Pullman Dover-bound 'Golden Arrow' in 1926.

As can be seen, there is no shortage of luxuriant tree growth in this part of south-east London as a Victoria to Kent Coast express, headed by EMU No 375305, climbs through Sydenham Hill 82 years later in November 2008. *MHCB collection/MHCB*

between a suburban and long-distance unit has become far less distinct, which is certainly a bonus for the suburban traveller, who may well find him or herself making a 10-minute journey between, say, New Cross and Waterloo or Richmond and Clapham Junction in exactly the same type of vehicle as someone up from the Kent, Sussex or Hampshire coasts. This has not always gone down well with the latter class of customer, with whom one has some sympathy. However, they might reflect that for every Pullman plying between Victoria, Brighton and Eastbourne, Charing Cross and Hastings or Waterloo and Bournemouth, there were very many times more hard-riding, draughty, uncomfortable carriages plying the same routes. The worst carriages today are infinitely better designed than the norm in pre-nationalisation and early BR days.

Stations, too, have improved. In the immediate post-war years many suburban ones were ramshackle, suffering from years of neglect, dirty and unfit for purpose. A few had real architectural merit, but others needed everything but the platforms demolishing and a fresh start made. Unfortunately the clasp-type structures that succeeded them, composed of pre-formed units that could be erected in various forms, were hardly any better. They were cheap and looked it. From the late 1980s a different attitude gradually became apparent; with more sensitive appreciation of the merits of adapting existing buildings to modern requirements, it became profitable for private enterprise to open refreshment and other facilities at locations where they had once been but were now long gone, or had never had them.

However, the ugly scourge of vandalism has become a threat, sometimes more perceived than real, but troubling for all that. Unstaffed stations do not help, and although security cameras are better than nothing, they are no substitute for the presence of a real, live railwayman. Some stations are in locations that will always seem unappealing and where no one would hang around longer than necessary – we can all think of our favourites in this category. Others are positively welcoming, a pleasure to spend time on: Kew and the extraordinary Elmstead Woods, with its gloriously abundant flora and rustic bridges over lily ponds, are two such.

Until the early 1960s many suburban stations possessed a goods yard where an elderly tank engine might be seen pottering around, indulging in a bit of light shunting before toddling off down the line to the next station. By this late date the whole set-up was an anachronism, losing the railways vast sums of money and getting in the way of passenger services. Today these yards are far more usefully employed as car parks, shopping centres, DIY stores and such like, quite often generating more business for the railway than the goods yard ever did.

Between 1899 and 1923 three railways performed the business south of the Thames: the London & South Western, the London, Brighton & South Coast, and the South Eastern & Chatham. All became part of the Southern Railway at the 'Grouping', and although this was absorbed by British Railways in 1948, it still kept its identity as the Southern Region. Travellers in a Southern suburban train in the early British Railways years might well find themselves in a carriage of pre-Grouping origin, the most likely alternative being one of Bulleid design. Indeed, for some years after 1948 Bulleid-designed EMUs continued to be built, and not only for Southern Region use. They carried large numbers of passengers and, with separate doors to each compartment, it was possible to load and unload speedily. Comfort and, in winter, warmth were not prime considerations. The revolutionary PEP of 1971 changed all that, leading to the automatic-sliding-door, open-layout EMUs that are now the norm.

Green for long seemed the only possible colour for a Southern EMU, until BR Rail Blue came in during the mid-1960s, followed by blue and grey; nowadays, with, as pre-1923, the network divided into three separate operating companies, a riot of attractive colour is the order of the day. Perhaps most pleasing is not just the revival of the name 'Southern' for the former Central Section lines, basically the old LB&SCR, but the painting of its trains in shades of green.

Michael H. C. Baker
Wareham, Dorset

South Western lines to Clapham Junction

WEST BYFLEET: A West of England express passes at speed on the long, straight stretch of quadruple track in the last days of the LSWR, c1920. The locomotive is No 447, one of Dugald Drummond's final class of 4-6-0. Nicknamed 'Paddleboxes' on account of the enormous splashers covering their 6ft 7in driving wheels, there were ten of these 'T14' Class four-cylinder locomotives, built in 1911-12. Better than Drummond's other locomotives of this design, they were nevertheless soon outmoded by Urie's much more modern successors. However, fitted with superheaters and with raised running plates they still found employment throughout Southern Railway days, No 447 being withdrawn by British Railways in 1951. The first four carriages of the train are non-corridor vehicles, but the rest appear to be corridor stock including a clerestory restaurant car.

West Byfleet in 2008 is still a deeply wooded part of what is now outer suburbia, and Class 455 EMUs will get commuters to Waterloo in 45 minutes. Approaching is a Class 450 EMU, built in Germany by Siemens and introduced by South West Trains for suburban and long-distance stopping duties in the early 2000s. The 455s were introduced in 1983. *MHCB collection/MHCB*

WEYBRIDGE station, just over 19 miles from Waterloo, is seen here around the turn of the 20th century looking towards London. Two tracks are sufficient for main-line traffic, and there is a bay platform on the down side.

In 2008, on the left is the up bay platform with a Class 450, which has just arrived from Waterloo via Virginia Water and Staines. There are now four tracks for the main line, only the outer ones having platform faces. The station has been much rebuilt, the booking office area, reached by steps, quite recently; it also offers refreshment facilities. The original booking office, situated beside the road bridge, remains, but is now a restaurant. *MHCB collection/MHCB*

HERSHAM is seen here in Southern Railway days, some time in the mid-1930s. Another long express is hauled, somewhat surprisingly for so late a date, by No 158, one of Drummond's 'L11' mixed-traffic 4-4-0s. Most of the carriages are modern Maunsell vehicles, the third one an LSWR-built dining car. With plenty of Urie and Maunsell 4-6-0s, as well as Maunsell 2-6-0s, available, there must have been huge demands on the motive power department if the best it could find was this elderly 1903-vintage mixed-traffic veteran.

Rather more appropriate motive power is this Siemens-built five-car Class 444 EMU speeding through Hersham past the trees that hide the houses beyond in the winter of 2008 on its way from Poole to Waterloo. The 45 Class 144s were built in Vienna and put into service by South West Trains between 2003 and 2005 on the Weymouth and Portsmouth routes. Their reliability was such that testing was cut short so that they could enter passenger service. *MHCB collection/MHCB*

SURBITON station is seen in the early years of the 20th century before electrification. It was known originally as Kingston upon Railway, and only got a station in 1838 when Kingston thought itself too snooty for such vulgar contrivances. Of course, Kingston later came to regret this, especially as it found itself on a branch, while Surbiton was on the main line. But such is life.

The second photograph shows Surbiton station today, looking towards London. The fastest trains take just 18 minutes to reach Waterloo. *MHCB collection/MHCB*

SURBITON: The exterior of the station is seen c1910 and some 100 years later. The Southern Railway embraced the Art Deco style with greater enthusiasm than any of the other 'Big Four' companies, and the new Surbiton station, completed just before the Second World War, is probably its best example. *MHCB collection/MHCB*

KINGSTON: The 'Kingston Loop' rejoins the main line at New Malden, having diverged at Clapham Junction. This is Kingston in March 1959, with 'M7' No 30043 shunting the goods yard. Many suburban stations still retained their goods yards at this time, most of their business being coal traffic. Smokeless zones helped to put paid to this, and British Railways was only too glad to be rid of such yards, a drain on its resources.

At the same location in July 2008 a Class 455 EMU is pulling out, having just crossed the Thames. The land occupied by suburban goods yards was either turned into commuter car parks or more often, as in Kingston's case, sold off for residential or commercial development. *Both MHCB*

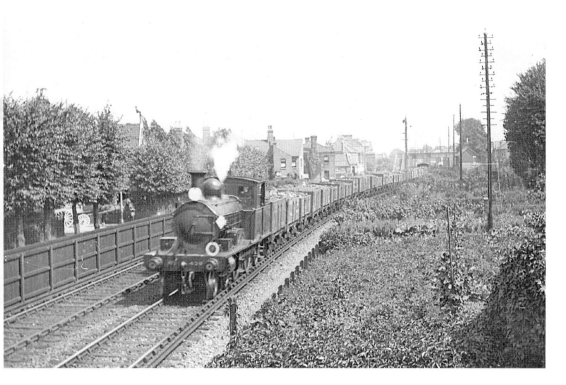

HOUNSLOW: The Hounslow loop runs between Barnes and Whitton Junction/Feltham Junction. Adams 4-4-2T No 429 heads a down goods on the Loop shortly after electrification, some time around 1918. Most of the class was withdrawn between 1921 and 1928, and this is the only picture I have ever seen of one working a freight train in the London area. It is difficult to be precise about the location, but just about the only curve on the line that would correspond to the rather vague details on the back of the unattributed print is just west of Hounslow station.

West of Hounslow on 12 March 2009 a Waterloo-bound Class 450 'Desiro' is approaching Hounslow station, hidden behind the trees. Immediately beneath the bridge from which the photograph was taken is Hounslow Junction, where the lines to Staines and Richmond diverge. *MHCB collection/MHCB*

RAYNES PARK: Back on the main line, 'N15X' No 2327 *Trevithick* passes Raynes Park with a down West of England express c1937. Originally 4-6-4Ts introduced by the LB&SCR in 1914, electrification of the Brighton and Eastbourne routes left this class of seven engines unemployed, so they were rebuilt as 4-6-0s in 1934-36 and transferred to the Western Section. Despite their new classification, suggesting that they were a variation on the 'N15' 'King Arthur' Class, they never reproduced the sparkle they had shown as 'Baltic' tanks and would only have been given the sort of top-link duty we see here at summer weekends.

In September 1955, in charge of another West of England express, is 'Merchant Navy' 'Pacific' No 35002 *Union Castle* in more or less original condition. It beggars belief that the powers that be could have been taken in by Bulleid's assertion that these 'Pacifics', when planned in the darkest days of the Second World War, could be classified as 'mixed traffic'. Any locomotive less suited to goods train haulage than a 'Merchant Navy', with its propensity to slip at the slightest opportunity, was surely never conceived and built. West of England expresses usually consisted of a vast number of sections, detached at various points in Devon and Cornwall, and this is no exception. The leading three-carriage set is an early Bulleid example, very similar to the EMU on the next track. On the left a 1925 Maunsell EMU is about to set off bound for Waterloo.

Finally, in May 2008 two Class 444 'Desiro' sets of South West Trains head westwards through Raynes Park. The up slow and fast line signals, although not the same ones, are in identical positions in all three pictures. *MHCB collection/MHCB (2)*

18

RAYNES PARK is hardly a compact station. The staggered up island platform begins opposite where the down slow line one ends, while the far platform face of the latter, serving the Chessington and Guildford via Epsom lines, is set on a pronounced curve. In this picture, dating from around 1910, an 'M7' 0-4-4T is arriving at the down Epsom line platform.

At the same location in February 2009 passengers have just alighted from a Chessington train, while in the distance a Class 455 bound for Woking is pulling into the down main line platform. The awnings have been rebuilt but the platforms are largely unaltered. *MHCB collection/MHCB*

Opposite page WIMBLEDON: No 525, an Adams 4-4-2T built in the 1880s for suburban traffic out of Waterloo, is performing just such a duty at Wimbledon c1902. These 4-4-2Ts were at this time being replaced by 'M7' 0-4-4Ts and sent off to work country branches. Many had been scrapped by 1923, but three lived on and on, working the Lyme Regis branch into BR days and ensuring that one, No 584, was preserved.

Wimbledon station has changed out of all recognition in the last century, so it is impossible to locate exactly where No 525 was standing. Today appearances by locomotive-hauled trains of any type at Wimbledon are rare indeed, but here is the veteran No 37612 passing through at the head of a departmental train in the summer of 2008. The English Electric Class 37s were introduced between 1960 and 1965 and proved to be one of the most successful of all British-built diesel designs. *Pamlin/MHCB*

WIMBLEDON: The line bringing the Metropolitan District Underground trains to Wimbledon was built by the LSWR in 1889 and used by that company and its successors for empty stock movements and during emergencies. Here on 1 August 1983 are four London Underground units, three D stock trains dating from 1980, and a much older one of basically pre-war design.

Refurbishment of the D stock has resulted in the welcome reappearance of colour on Underground trains – red fronts and blue stripes. Combined with the blue and yellow fronts and the brilliant red sides of South West Trains' refurbished Class 455s, a black and white photograph scarcely does justice to the Wimbledon scene in 2008. The platforms could do with a bit of weeding. *Both MHCB*

WIMBLEDON: A branch line with a character all its own was that linking Wimbledon and West Croydon via Mitcham. Much of it was single track through a surprisingly rural landscape and worked by two-coach EMUs, known as the '2' trains. 2EPB No 5773 is seen at platform 10 in 1972.

Twenty-five years later No 456024 is seen wearing the short-lived, attractive grey and yellow livery of Connex. There are 24 of these units, delivered in 1991. Extensive redevelopment has taken place around the station.

Trains ceased running over the Wimbledon to West Croydon line in May 1997, and three years later, in May 2000, Tramlink (Croydon) took over, bringing trams back to Wimbledon for the first time in almost 50 years. Built by Bombardier and almost identical to those running in Cologne, tram No 2539 stands at platform 10 soon after its entry into service. *All MHCB*

DURNSFORD ROAD, WIMBLEDON:
When the LSWR began its electrified service between Waterloo and Wimbledon via East Putney in October 1915, power was provided by its own generating station at Durnsford Road. A depot was also built here. On 23 August 1958 immaculate 'Lord Nelson' Class 4-6-0 No 30854 *Howard of Effingham* has charge of empty boat train stock, much of it dating back to the 1920s, bound for Southampton.

In the second photograph a two-car EMU unit, No 4543, formed of two former LB&SCR arc-roof motor coaches, converted by the Southern Railway from steam stock in the late 1920s, shunts at the entrance to Durnsford Road depot in the early 1950s. A Bulleid 4SUB is heading along the down slow line.

In September 2008 two Class 455s head past Durnsford Road on the down slow line. The power station is long gone and the depot has been completely rebuilt, although some of the track layout remains unaltered. *All MHCB*

Opposite page DURNSFORD ROAD, WIMBLEDON: The prototype PEP unit was a huge leap forward in thinking for Southern suburban stock, at last doing away with slam doors and introducing a layout far more suitable for short-distance journeys. From it was developed the production Class 508 EMUs. PEP No 4001 stands at Durnsford Road in January 1979.

Now renamed Wimbledon Train Care Depot, departmental vehicles are seen in September 2008 with, over on the right, one of the somewhat problematic Class 458 JOP Alsthom units of 2001. *Both MHCB*

EARLSFIELD is the next station up the line towards Clapham Junction. 'Schools' Class 4-4-0 No 30913 *Christ's Hospital* is approaching with the 6.22am from Bournemouth to Waterloo on 6 June 1961, with the chimneys of Durnsford Road power station looming in the background. A number of 'Schools' Class engines, made redundant by the first stage of the Kent Coast electrification, had moved over to the Western Section in 1959. Just over a week after this picture was taken, the Kent Coast electrification second stage was completed, signalling the end of the 'Schools' Class, among many others. *Christ's Hospital* was withdrawn in January 1962 and the entire class, apart from three preserved examples, would be gone by the end of that year.

In October 2008 an eight-coach train, 'Desiro' unit No 450038 leading, approaches Earlsfield on an Alton to Waterloo working, while another 'Desiro' heads towards Wimbledon on the down fast line. *Both MHCB*

EARLSFIELD: While many of the 'M7' 0-4-4Ts, designed for suburban traffic in and out of Waterloo, migrated to the country on electrification, a number remained at Nine Elms for empty stock Waterloo workings, mostly only as far as Clapham yards but sometimes, as here, further afield. On 6 June 1961 No 30248 has worked up a fair turn of speed with a long train of corridor stock and is passing a 1925-built suburban EMU, augmented with two all-steel Bulleid trailer carriages, at the east end of Earlsfield station.

A Waterloo to Exeter express headed by DMU No 159006 approaches Earlsfield on 12 February 2009. Various pieces of lineside apparatus beyond the platform mean that a telephoto view is essential today. *Both MHCB*

NEAR EARLSFIELD: With the chimneys of Durnsford Road power station faintly visible on the horizon, 'Lord Nelson' 4-6-0 No 30856 *Lord St Vincent* heads through the cutting between Earlsfield and Clapham Junction with an up Ocean Liner Express from Southampton on 2 June 1959. Two bogie vans are provided for passengers' luggage, while the eighth vehicle is a former Pullman painted in Southern Region green.

An eight-coach up semi-fast service composed of two Class 450 units passes the same spot in October 2008. In the intervening 49 years the telegraph poles have disappeared and the bushes and trees have moved much further down the cutting sides. Set deep among the trees above the cutting on the up side are the remains, carefully preserved by the Wandsworth Society, of a windmill that the LSWR erected in the 1830s to pump water from the cutting into a lake known as the Black Sea. It ceased work in 1870 when the lake was filled in. Presumably by then either flooding of the railway was no longer a problem or an alternative method had been found of disposing of the water. *Both MHCB*

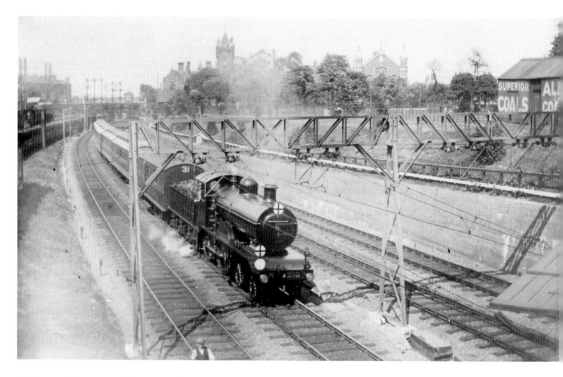

Clapham Junction

CLAPHAM JUNCTION: Seen from the south, No 210, a 'B2x' 4-4-0 of 1898 rebuilt with a Marsh boiler, heads the LB&SCR's Royal Train of clerestory carriages, built in 1897, on the down fast line c1910. On the left are the LSWR's

tracks. The station was opened, jointly, by the LSWR and the LB&SCR in 1863, although the first trains to pass through were those of the London & Southampton Railway, the LSWR's predecessor, in 1838; the area was not at that time considered busy enough to warrant a station. The population grew enormously in the second half of the 19th century, from 6,000 in 1840 to 168,000 by 1910.

At the same location today are a Southern Class 337 EMU and a South West Trains Class 444 'Desiro' in the distance. Strictly speaking the station should be called Battersea Junction as it is in Battersea, which was a distinctly working-class area; but nearby Clapham was considered somewhat more up-market, so that name was chosen. *MHCB collection/MHCB*

CLAPHAM JUNCTION: A close-up of the Clapham Yard sidings in the summer of 1988. This was the period when the 5WES York-built 'Wessex Electrics' were entering service. From left to right are some buffer cars from their REP predecessors, 4TC unit No 8024, some BR Mark I sleeping cars – of which the Southern certainly had no need – inspection carriage DS71055 converted from a Maunsell Hastings line vehicle, and prototype PEP No 4002.

In June 2008 Class 444 and 450 'Desiros' dominate the scene with, on the left, one of the Class 458 4JOP EMUs intended for the Reading line and introduced in 2001. *Both MHCB*

CLAPHAM JUNCTION: No 30741 *Joyous Gard*, one of the original LSWR-built, Urie-designed 'N15' 4-6-0s of 1918 incorporated into the 'King Arthur' Class by the Southern Railway, swings its Southampton-bound express through Clapham Junction in 1952.

At the same spot in April 2008 South West Trains 'Desiro' No 444029 is bound for Poole. *Brian Morrison/MHCB*

CLAPHAM JUNCTION: Because the traction motors of the 4REPs were being reconditioned for use in the new 5WES units, there was a period in 1988 when all sorts of makeshift formations were in use, and here we see a Class 73 hauling a Weymouth to Waterloo express, the first two carriages of which are a Brake 1st and a restaurant car, not surprisingly attracting the attention of the trainspotters on the platform end at Clapham Junction.

Steam can still be seen at Clapham Junction from time to time. 'Battle of Britain' 'Pacific' No 34067 *Tangmere* takes the up fast Central Section line on its way to Victoria after a round trip through Staines, Guildford, Redhill and East Croydon in May 2004. *Both MHCB*

CLAPHAM JUNCTION: The 3SUBs of 1925 were purely suburban units. No 4352, with an additional all-steel Bulleid trailer, heads through Clapham Junction on the Western Section down slow line in about 1956.

A little later the Southern Railway introduced 33 4LAV units for semi-fast and stopping services on the electrified London to Brighton line. The Southern never built any steam-hauled non-corridor stock, at least from new, but if it had it would no doubt have looked very like a 4LAV trailer. The 4LAVs served faithfully for more than 35 years, almost all of their efforts being confined to the Victoria and London Bridge to Brighton line. No 2924 brings up the rear of an eight-coach train passing Clapham Junction on its way to Victoria in about 1966.

The 5WES 'Wessex Electrics' were probably the most comfortable of all EMUs to run on Southern lines. Based on the Mark 3 bodyshell, these 75ft 6in-long carriages, formed into five-car units, were a great improvement on anything experienced in this part of the world before. Two 5WESs in their original livery head past Clapham Junction on an express working from Weymouth to Waterloo in 1990. They now operate for Southern. *Colour-Rail (2)/MHCB*

Right The Parcels Office at Clapham Junction, photographed in 2009. *MHCB*

CLAPHAM JUNCTION: Few lines can have experienced such great variations in passenger traffic as the West London line through Kensington Olympia. In 1965 the only regular passenger service was a rush-hour one to and from Clapham Junction, mainly for Post Office workers. In this picture a BR Standard 2-6-4T is running around its train having brought it into platform 1.

Since then the importance of this cross-London link has steadily increased and today it is used by long-distance trains as well as regular London Overground ones running between Clapham Junction and Willesden Junction. A Southern Class 377 EMU is on its way from the Sussex coast to Watford Junction. *Both MHCB*

Waterloo

NINE ELMS was the principal motive power depot serving Waterloo. 'King Arthur' Class 4-6-0 No 30788 *Sir Urre of the Mount* is seen there in July 1961.

With the end of steam Nine Elms was demolished and replaced by London's principal fruit and vegetable market. On Sundays car boot sales are also held there, although I doubt if a 'King Arthur' ever comes up for sale...
Both MHCB

VAUXHALL: In July 1961 'Schools' 4-4-0 No 30910 *Merchant Taylors* heads a Waterloo-Lymington Pier express, passing No 30918 *Hurstpierpoint* backing down to Waterloo to take out a down express.

In about 1962 a 12-coach Waterloo to Portsmouth Harbour express is headed by 4COR No 3141. Full electric services between Waterloo and Portsmouth began in July 1937. Four-coach units, instead of the six-car ones that had been used for the Central Section Sussex Coast services, were now standard, with corridor connections between each unit. This gave rise to the nickname 'Nelsons', both because of the Portsmouth connection and their 'one-eyed' look, obvious here, although we trainspotters at Clapham Junction used the somewhat derogatory term 'Belly-wobblers', on account of the movement of the leading corridor connection as the trains swung around the curves. The Houses of Parliament provide an unmistakable backdrop.

As steam gradually faded out in 1966/67 Class 47 diesel-electric locomotives sometimes appeared on the 'Bournemouth Belle', as here seen (*above right*) heading through Vauxhall in 1966. A BR Mark 1 bogie van is provided for luggage.

With the advent of Eurostar from Waterloo International in November 1994 such exotic sights as this (*right*) could be seen at Vauxhall: a Waterloo to Paris express alongside a Class 455 EMU bound for Chessington South. *All MHCB*

WATERLOO: On the extreme right of this 1990 view is preserved 2BIL No 2090, on the adjacent track is a Class 33 diesel-electric locomotive, and a collection of EMUs in the sidings on the far left-hand, Windsor line, side – a scene that would shortly be transformed.

A most elegant and award-winning station, Waterloo International, was built on the site of the Windsor line platforms and opened in November 1994. Three Eurostars are seen in the station while a South West Trains Class 455 departs.

With the opening of the direct Eurostar line from the Channel Tunnel to St Pancras International, Waterloo International closed in November 2007. A Class 456 8JOP is pulling out on a Reading service in October 2008, while the International station stands sadly empty. *All MHCB*

Right Celebrations to mark the last day of Eurostars from Waterloo on 13 November 2007, before transferring business to St Pancras International. *MHCB*

WATERLOO: In about 1900, before the extensive rebuilding programme began, which was not completed until after the First World War, we see LSWR Adams 'Jubilee' 'A12' Class 0-4-2 No 645 of 1887. The very last locomotives of this wheel arrangement at work in the UK, two survived long enough to be taken over by British Railways.

In January 1956 'M7' 0-4-4T No 124 and 'King Arthur' 4-6-0 No 30457 *Sir Bedivere* stand at Waterloo. Once employed on suburban passenger trains, the 'M7s' were a familiar sight at Waterloo for more than 50 years, latterly spending much of their time working empty stock trains in and out of the terminus. *Sir Bedevere* was one of the first batch of 'N15' Class 'King Arthurs', brought out by Maunsell in 1925, a development of Urie's 'N15s' of 1918, and built at Eastleigh.

In 2004 Class 66 No 66068 is at Waterloo. Locomotives are a rare sight at the terminus today, multiple units having a complete monopoly of day-to-day passenger work, but this EWS diesel-electric Co-Co was employed on Sunday engineering work. *NRM/MHCB (2)*

WATERLOO: In this view from the footbridge linking Waterloo East and Waterloo Main Line stations, a train of EPBs, with No 3207 bringing up the rear, heads for Charing Cross in 1989.

At the same location in May 2008, South Eastern 'Networkers' Nos 465002 and 465164 are coming and going. *Both MHCB*

Charing Cross, Holborn Viaduct and London Bridge

CHARING CROSS is the closest main-line station to the heart of the West End, being within sight of Trafalgar Square. Opened by the South Eastern Railway on 11 January 1864 close to the blacking factory where Charles Dickens worked as a boy – rather appropriately, for it served the Kent he knew so well – it has six platform faces and brings in enormous numbers of commuters each day. It used to be relatively quiet at weekends – well, perhaps not in summer with holiday traffic to the Kent Coast and the continent – but with the opening up of shops seven days a week and so many leisure and aesthetic attractions within walking distance, there is scarcely ever a quite moment at Charing Cross. In about 1920, No 4, a Stirling 4-4-0 rebuilt by Wainwright, is about to leave with its train of non-corridor carriages, the leading Brake 3rd having the distinctive 'birdcage' guard's lookout, just like the carriage on the opposite platform.

In 1990 a complete rebuilding, or rather a totally new construction above the platforms, resulted in a pretty gloomy atmosphere down below and a rather splendid-looking post-modern structure above, incorporating office and shopping accommodation. As can be seen, certain features from the old station were retained. 4CIG No 1871 is ready to depart for the Kent Coast in 1991. The CIGs were originally designed to replace the Brighton line express units in the late 1960s, but many also worked on the Eastern and Western Sections before they finally disappeared in 2005.

In December 2007 we see No 376827, a 'Suburban Electrostar' EMU, one of 36 four-car units introduced in 2005/6 and operated by South Eastern. *MHCB collection/MHCB (2)*

CHARING CROSS STATION. FOLKESTONE EXPRESS.

CHARING CROSS: The height of late Victorian fashion at Charing Cross, as passengers board the clerestory-roofed Pullmans of the 'Folkestone Express'.

Despite the smiles, travel in Bulleid's experimental double-deck EMU of 1949, seen here in a publicity photograph

taken at Charing Cross, was about as far removed in comfort from a Victorian Pullman as can be imagined. Designed to carry 1,060 passengers in the eight-car train, compared to some 770 in two contemporary 4SUBs, the brave experiment failed on several counts; conditions, especially in the upper section, were cramped and stuffy, and loading and unloading took so long that any advantage gained by the extra capacity was lost. We schoolboys nevertheless took great delight in a ride in one whenever possible, and to give the units their due they remained in regular service for more than 20 years, not being withdrawn until October 1971. One or two coaches have been preserved, but are in a sorry state. *Commercial postcard, MHCB collection/MHCB*

HOLBORN VIADUCT station is seen here in about 1955. It was opened by the London, Chatham & Dover Railway in March 1874 to serve the City of London, and in later years almost all its traffic was suburban. It closed in January 1990 when the Snow Hill line was reinstated as a passenger route; the underground City Thameslink replaced Holborn Viaduct station.

Instead of passing over Ludgate Hill, the reinstated Snow Hill line descends quite steeply immediately north of Blackfriars station and into a tunnel – which, incidentally, at last gave an unrestricted view of St Paul's Cathedral from Fleet Street and Ludgate Circus. A Southern Railway Class 319 EMU is seen descending towards City Thameslink in February 2009. *Both MHCB*

ELEPHANT & CASTLE station was across the Thames south of Holborn Viaduct. In about 1930 'T9' No E3207 heads a lightweight train from Holborn Viaduct to Maidstone East. A number of these efficient and long-lived LSWR built 4-4-0s were transferred by the Southern Railway to the Eastern Section, although just why is not entirely clear given that there was already a large number of native 4-4-0s available for work there.

At the same location in October 2008 is South Eastern 'Networker' No 465188. The wooden platforms have been replaced, although the wall remains, albeit painted; the overall roofs has gone, destroyed in the Blitz, and a post war block of flats has appeared. *MHCB collection/MHCB*

LONDON BRIDGE: Former SE&CR 'C' Class 0-6-0 No 31513 approaches London Bridge with a train of vans c1955. One of the most useful engines inherited by the Southern Railway, the SE&CR built 109 of them between 1900 and 1908, and although principally goods engines they did a good deal of passenger work too. All but three of the 'C' Class passed into British Railways hands and the last was not withdrawn until the mid-1960s, being now preserved and at work on the Bluebell Railway.

In 1971 a Class 33 diesel-electric is about to couple up to its Oxted line commuter train while EPB EMUs are arriving or departing. London Bridge is one of London's oldest stations, dating back to 1836 when the London & Greenwich Railway opened, which became the South Eastern Railway. A little later the London & Croydon Railway arrived and would eventually become part of the London, Brighton & South Coast Railway. Ever since, London Bridge has consisted of two distinct sections, the Brighton or Central Section side being a terminus, while the platforms on the other side, numbers 1-6, serve through lines on which trains continue to Cannon Street, Blackfriars and beyond, or Charing Cross.

The third view shows the approach to the South Eastern (through) platforms in 2008. On the left are Class 376s, in the centre Class 465 'Networkers', and on the far right a Southern Class 377 heading for one of the terminal platforms. *Brian Morrison/MHCB (2)*

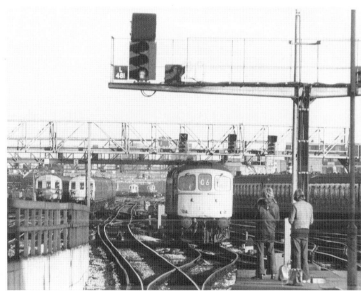

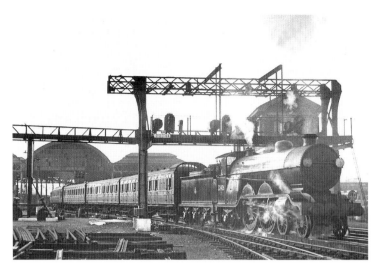

LONDON BRIDGE: In 1952 one of the celebrated Brighton 'Atlantics', No 32426 *St Alban's Head*, pulls out of London Bridge with an Oxted line train, which will eventually terminate at Brighton. The leading three carriages are an ex-SE&CR 'birdcage' set, coupled to Maunsell corridors. The very last 'Atlantics' in service in the UK, the 'H2s' of 1911 were a development of the 'H1s' of 1905, which their designer, Earle Marsh, had based on the GNR 'Atlantics', since he had previously been employed at Doncaster.

Being so near the docks, London Bridge station was badly damaged by bombing during the Second World War, the hotel, which had become offices, being totally destroyed. The station was eventually rebuilt, this being completed in December 1978 to the design of the BR Southern architect N. D. T. Wikeley, and the platforms on the Brighton side were extended; thus this picture is taken from roughly the same position as the previous one. Prominent in this November 1979 picture is 4CIG express unit No 7324, a type introduced in 1964, with suburban EPBs on the right.

The only regular scheduled non-electric service in and out of London Bridge today is that serving Uckfield – the section from there to Lewes and on to Brighton was closed in the 1960s, although over the years there have been several campaigns to get it reopened. In January 2009 four-car DMU No 171806 is about to depart. Six of these four-car units and six two-car Class 170/7 units were introduced by Southern in 2003/4, a great improvement on the long-serving and uncomfortable 'Thumper' DEMUs they replaced. *Brian Morrison/MHCB (2)*

LONDON BRIDGE: the 'past' picture was taken shortly after the inauguration of the extension of the third rail to the Sussex Coast in 1933. Three of the massive 6PUL motor coaches pose at the head of trains for (from left to right) Eastbourne, Worthing and Littlehampton, and Brighton. Although very well-appointed internally, the riding of the 6PULs left much to be desired. The letters 'PUL' indicated that refreshments were provided by an all-steel Pullman dining car.

The PULs, and the similar 6PAN units, which had a pantry car of SR design instead of a Pullman, but which was staffed by Pullman employees, were replaced by the 4CIGs and 4BIGS in the mid-1960s, and these in turn gave way to Southern Class 377s in 2005/6, one of which is seen at London Bridge in 2008. Surrounded as it is by some pretty tall buildings, these will seem very small beer when the Shard London Bridge, on which work has just started on the south-west corner of the site, near the bus terminus, is completed, for it will be the tallest skyscraper in Western Europe. *MHCB collection/MHCB*

North Kent lines to Dartford

NEW CROSS GATE is the first station out of London Bridge on the Brighton line (it acquired the suffix 'Gate' in SR days). Since 1869 it has also been the terminus of the East London Line, worked by the Underground under the Thames by way of Brunel's tunnel from Whitechapel. In this view, taken in 1952, one of the London Transport Bo-Bo electric locomotives, No 2 *Thomas Lord*, has just arrived with a train of Metropolitan Line compartment carriages on a rail tour that will head on down the Southern, steam-hauled.

The Underground service from Whitechapel to both New Cross Gate and New Cross was suspended in 2008 so that the extensive works needed to extend the trains over Southern tracks to West Croydon as part of the Overground network could be carried out. At the same location in September 2008 the Underground tracks having been temporarily removed while work on the extension is in progress. *MHCB collection/MHCB*

NEW CROSS GATE: An East London Line Underground train composed of clerestory-roofed stock dating from the 1920s arrives at New Cross Gate in 1969, passing a Southern Class 73 electro-diesel locomotive.
  In November 2008 EMU No 508210 has just passed under the newly erected bridge that will carry the East London up line over the London Bridge tracks. *Both MHCB*

NEW CROSS DEPOT was an important shed on the LB&SCR network, particularly in the days before electrification. In this view, dating from the days of the 'improved green' (ie yellow ochre) livery early in the Edwardian era, a fine selection of tank engines of Stroudley and Billinton origin stand in front of the shed.

The shed closed in 1948 and today a Sainsbury's superstore stands on its site. *MHCB collection/MHCB*

NEW CROSS Looking towards London Bridge in 1970, EPB No 5209 heads an eight-coach train on the down through line while another eight-car EPB trains is at the up platform alongside. The differing roof-lines of the EPB carriages will be noticed. The second view, from October 2008, shows two Charing Cross-bound EMUs. *Brian Morrison/MHCB*

NEW CROSS: On the approach to New Cross from London Bridge during an evening rush hour in 1969, from left to right we see BR-design 2EPB No 5704 of 1951 at the head of a 10-coach suburban train, a Hastings 12-car express composed of two six-car diesel-electric flat-sided units dating from 1957/8 and headed by No 1031, Southern Railway-design 4EPB No 5045 of 1951, and another two-car EPB, No 5725, at the head of a 10-coach train.

At the same location in October 2008 are two eight-car electric trains, on the left 'Suburban Electrostar' No 376026 dating from 2005/6, and on the right 'Networker' No 465048 dating from 1993. *Both MHCB*

GROVE STREET, DEPTFORD, was one of the relatively few locations in the UK where railway tracks ran along a public road, in this instance giving the railway access to Deptford Wharf. The locomotive is a former LB&SCR 'E1' Class 0-6-0T, and the date c1948.

In Grove Street in February 2009 the Victorian terraces have been swept way and only at the far end of the street, close to the river, is there any indication of where a railway once ran, although the elderly lady may well remember those days. *MHCB collection/MHCB*

GREENWICH: An SR-design 4EPB leaves for Dartford in 1980. Originally the terminus of the first railway in London, the handsome station buildings, designed by George Smith and dating back to 1840, are now listed and have recently been sensitively restored.

In 2008 a 'Networker' is leaving for Dartford. Seemingly unchanged, this is deceptive, for behind the photographer there are now the recently opened platforms for the Docklands Light Railway.

Having moved to the London end of the up platform, we see on the right a Docklands Light Railway train bound for Lewisham arriving, having emerged from under the Thames, with a Cannon Street-bound 'Networker' in the distance on the left. *All MHCB*

CHARLTON station is on the North Kent line through Greenwich to Dartford and, just below Charlton Athletic's ground, sported this neat little signal box at Charlton Lane Crossing in 1970. A Class 37 is passing at the head of a down freight.

Remarkably, the signal box is still there today. In September 2008 an up Charing Cross-bound Class 356 unit has just passed. *Brian Morrison/MHCB*

SLADE GREEN: A Class 56 passes Slade Green depot with an up freight in 1985. The depot was built shortly after the amalgamation of the South Eastern and the London, Chatham & Dover Railways when it proved impossible to extend Bricklayers Arms depot, near London Bridge. Plenty of land was available on the marshes at Crayford on the Thames Estuary, and the depot opened in 1901. Converted to house electric multiple units by the Southern Railway in 1924, lines of EPBs can be seen in the sidings on both sides of the through lines.

A 'Networker' pulls out of the depot in March 2009. The lines heading off to the right immediately in front of the train are those of the Dartford Loop. Work on an extensive rebuild of the depot to accommodate the Eurostar fleet was completed in 1991. *Brian Morrison/MHCB*

ST JOHN'S is just beyond New Cross. An eight-coach train of two 4EPB units, led by No 5486, arrives at the up platform in 1985. All but the first carriage are in an experimental livery; originally painted in SR green, the EPBs later acquired Rail Blue and, from 1980, blue and grey. The last were withdrawn in March 1995.

Another eight-coach train, headed by No 375906, passes on up the fast line in September 2008. St John's, surrounded by some well-cared-for, attractive Victorian terraces and semi-detached houses, is rather curiously situated in that it has no direct road access, being reached by a footbridge from St John's Vale. The island platform serving the up and down fast lines was demolished in the 1970s, allowing track reorganisation. *Brian Morrison/MHCB*

ST JOHN'S: Viewed a few hundred yards nearer London Bridge, a Class 37 heads a freight in 1985, while in October 2008 an EMU passes. *Brian Morrison/MHCB*

SIDCUP: In 1955 'N1' No 31880, a three-cylinder 2-6-0 introduced by the SE&CR in 1922, heads past the signal box at the east end of the station with an up freight .

By 2008 the signal box and goods yard have disappeared, the latter replaced by a luxuriant growth of trees. A London-bound 'Networker' is entering the station. *Brian Morrison/MHCB*

DARTFORD: In November 1991 a 4EPB has just arrived from Victoria via Bexleyheath and will shortly return.

In February 2009 it is no longer possible to put one's head out of the windows of suburban EMUs, so we move back a little way down the platform to capture a 'Networker' on a Victoria train. Otherwise little seems to have changed to either the station or the immediate vicinity; even the gas holder remains. *Both MHCB*

Former SE&CR lines to Surrey and Kent

PECKHAM RYE: In 1951 newly introduced BR-designed 2EPB No 5708, working the South London line from Victoria to London Bridge, passes the EMU depot.

In April 2008 housing occupies the site of the depot as two-car Southern EMU No 456001 swings round on the line from Tulse Hill and North and East Dulwich. *R. C. Riley/MHCB*

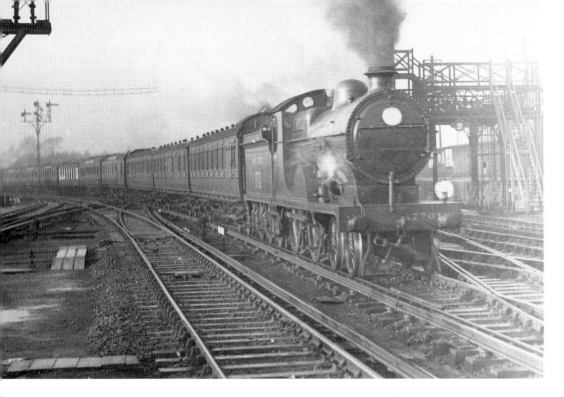

HERNE HILL: In about 1930 SE&CR-built 'L' Class 4-4-0 No 1770 approaches the station with a Victoria to Ramsgate express. The first three carriages are a non-corridor 'birdcage' set followed by a rake of Maunsell corridor carriages, the sixth vehicle being a Pullman. There were 12 of these powerful 4-4-0s, built in 1914, some of them by Borsig of Germany and delivered just before the outbreak of war. The line from the right comes in from Blackfriars and Holborn Viaduct.

A Brussels-bound Eurostar curves round towards Herne Hill 13 November 2007. This was the last day that Eurostar operated out of Waterloo and on the third rail. The next day services were transferred to St Pancras and the brand new dedicated route through Stratford and under the Thames. *MHCB collection/MHCB*

BROMLEY SOUTH: A 4VEP pulls away from Bromley South on its way from the Kent Coast to Victoria in 1975. Introduced in 1967 for the Bournemouth electrification, further batches were sent to the Central and Eastern Sections. Very popular with the operating authorities on account of their high seating capacity and the fact that they could operate both long-distance stopping and, if pushed, express services, they were heartily disliked by the travelling public for these very reasons. Draughty and uncomfortable, they long outstayed their welcome, the last not disappearing from ordinary service until 2006.

This September 2008 picture demonstrates what a dramatic growth there has been in the trees in the locality in the intervening 33 years. A 'Networker' is on its way to Victoria. *Both MHCB*

BROMLEY SOUTH: No 71012, one of the distinctive electric locomotives built at Doncaster in 1958 for the Kent Coast electrification is working light approaching Bromley South in 1975. The pantograph was for working in goods yard where the third rail would have been dangerous. The Class 71s had all been withdrawn by the end of 1977, although one, No E5001, has been preserved.

An Orpington-bound 'Networker' is seen at the same location in September 2008. *Both MHCB*

NEAR BROMLEY SOUTH: 'West Country' 'Pacific' No 34017 *Ilfracombe* is between Shortlands and Bromley South with the down 'Kentish Belle' all-Pullman train in about 1956. 4SUB No 4357 is heading towards Victoria on the up slow line.

At the same location on a wet September morning in 2008 'Networker' No 465919 curves towards Shortlands station on its way to Victoria. *Stanley Creer/MHCB*

BICKLEY is the next station east of Bromley South. On 12 July 1958 'E1' Class 4-4-0 No 31497 gets a grip on a Kent Coast holiday express. The set of Maunsell carriages, No 465, is the one seen on page 63 hauled by the 'L' Class 4-4-0. The Southern kept a relatively large fleet of elderly carriages for just such traffic, which spent all but a few days of the year vegetating in sidings all over the system. Accountants and aerosol cans put an end to this practice. The 'D1s' and 'E1s', rebuilds between 1919 and 1927 of Wainwright 'D' and 'E' Class locomotives, were fine engines, free running and, for a 4-4-0, powerful and consequently considered well able to work alongside Bulleid 'Pacifics' on holiday expresses right down to electrification in 1959/61.

The archaic-looking arc-roof former LB&SCR 4SUBs (converted from locomotive-hauled stock by the Southern Railway) outlived both their SE&CR and LSWR contemporaries. In the second picture No 4504, coupled to a Bulleid 4SUB, heads out of Bickley towards Orpington on 23 August 1958. Another one can just be seen entering Bickley station.

Finally, South Eastern EMU No 375814 heads an eight-coach train from Victoria to the Kent Coast past Bickley in June 2008. Semaphore signals have long disappeared, and the track layout has been altered so the outermost lines are now the fast ones. *All MHCB*

BICKLEY: In August 1961 'L' Class 4-4-0 No 31780 is seen in charge of down holiday express.

A 'Networker' arrives at Bickley in May 2008. There are still signal gantries, but not surprisingly the water tower has gone, as have the goods sidings on the up side. *Both MHCB*

ELMSTEAD WOODS, north-east of Bromley on the line through Hither Green and Chislehurst to the Kent Coast, can lay claim to being the most attractive suburban station anywhere in the London area. The buildings date from 1904 when the line was quadrupled. A Kent Coast express, headed by 4CEP No 7129, is emerging from the tunnel on the down fast line. A cutting would have been a cheaper option, but the landowner insisted on a tunnel.

Set in a deep cutting in a wooded, affluent area, the architecture is attractive in its own right, but what makes Elmstead Woods so outstanding is the riot of greenery, especially on the 40-foot-wide centre island platform, complete with ponds and rustic bridges. I had travelled through it a number of times without alighting and it was only when making a special journey in connection with this

book that I fully discovered its delights – a great credit to the dedicated staff who tend it with such loving care. 'Networker' No 465177 pulls out on its way to Victoria in October 2008. *Brian Morrison/ MHCB*

ELMERS END station was opened by the South Eastern Railway in 1864, with the line to Hayes, then deep in the country, following in 1882. In 1988 two-car 'Networker' No 466023 stands in the bay platform on the right with an Addiscombe train while opposite is a Hayes to Charing Cross service.

At the same location in 2008 a tram, about to depart for East Croydon, now occupies the bay platform, which has been resurfaced and the awning extended. *Both MHCB*

ADDISCOMBE was the terminus of a branch from Elmers End, and it was originally intended that the line would continue the mile and a half to East Croydon, but this never happened and it remained something of a backwater. *Teenage Rebel*, the film being advertised in this 1957 view at the Davis, Croydon's largest and now vanished cinema, was one of the last made by Ginger Rogers.

In 1997 Networker No 466028 stands at the platform at Addiscombe. Very little would seem to have changed apart from the installation of an automatic ticket machine and an accumulation of rubbish.

Trains ceased to serve Addiscombe in 1997 in preparation for the inauguration of Croydon Tramlink, which would take over most of the trackbed of the Addiscombe branch. This is the same location as the previous picture, the long brick wall being about the only surviving structure from the station. *All MHCB*

ADDISCOMBE CARRIAGE SHED is seen in 1996, by then disused with a sign prohibiting 'Networkers' from using it, and gradually being engulfed by the undergrowth. The same location in July 2008 is now the Addiscombe Railway Park. *Both MHCB*

BINGHAM ROAD is on the line from Elmers End to Sanderstead, which, branching off from the Addisombe line at Woodside, was also very much a backwater. Bingham Road opened as a halt in July 1906, closed in March 1915, was reopened as a new station when the line was electrified in 1935, and finally gave up the ghost in May 1983. Although the line was sometimes used by through holiday trains and excursions to the coast travelling a roundabout route via Elmers End and the Oxted line, services gradually declined until they ceased in 1983. Bingham Road achieved fame in 1961 when the Tony Hancock film, *The Rebel*, used it as a location for several sequences, it being ideal on account of the paucity of train services.

Tramlink, opened in 2000, runs over much of the Elmers End to Sanderstead line. This is the Addiscombe stop in May 2008, occupying the site of Bingham Road station, it and the embankment upon which it stood, having been demolished. *Both MHCB*

COOMBE LANE TUNNEL: A BR-design 2EPB emerges from Coombe Lane Tunnel between Bingham Road and Coombe Road on 26 April 1983. The line ran beside Lloyd Park and on one edge of this was the last farm within the County Borough of Croydon. Our school's cross-country run used to pass through the farmyard; cross-country running was not my thing, so my friend Cyril and I managed to obtain employment as markers, pointing the way for those rather more dedicated athletes. One Saturday afternoon – this would have been in 1950 – we were leaning over the pig sty, tickling the ear of a friendly porker and chatting to the pig man who had quite a pronounced, rural accent. 'Where are you from?' we asked. 'Lived here all my life, man and boy,' was the reply. He must have been one of the very last with a genuine Croydon as opposed to a South London accent.

Two Tramlink cars are seen at the same location beside Lloyd Park in 2002, the tunnel mouth obscured by the tram disappearing into the distance. The tram tracks, instead of continuing on to Sanderstead, swing to the right here up alongside Lloyd Park and parallel to Coombe Road, over the top of Shirley Hills, down past Addington village and up the North Downs to windy New Addington. *Both MHCB*

SELSDON: A New Cross to Hastings excursion approaches Selsdon station (beyond which the line from Elmers End joined the Oxted line) hauled by 'L1' Class 4-4-0 No 31788 on 12 June 1949. There were 15 'L1s', a post-Grouping development of the 'L' Class, introduced in 1926 and, until the arrival of the 'Schools' Class, the principal Hastings line passenger locomotives.

In February 2009 a builder's yard occupied the site of the previous photograph. However, not only does the Downton Road footbridge in the background of the 'past' picture still survive but it is possible to make out from the footbridge some track and points, a valuable collection of forgotten scrap metal. Trains continued to use an oil terminal at Selsdon, connected to the Oxted line, until 1993. *MHCB collection/MHCB*

SELSDON: 'K' Class 2-6-0 No 32344 climbs the bank from South Croydon through Selsdon on 18 February 195?
with the 3.52pm Victoria to East Grinstead. This section of Selsdon station had a very neglected air, with only
three trains a day calling there, and even these would cease after 14 June that year. The 17 'K' Class engines, built
by the LB&SCR between 1913 and 1921, were the principal freight locomotives on the Brighton line until the end
of steam, but they did from time to time appear on passenger trains. Unusually No 32344 is carrying headlamps
rather than white discs – perhaps there was fog about. The first three carriages are Bulleid corridors, which were
beginning to be cascaded on to the Oxted line at this time, replacing the SE&CR 'birdcage' non-corridors.

Building work, growth of bushes and fear of prosecution made it impossible to take photographs from the same
side of the tracks as the 'past' picture. However, by poking the camera through a fence on the other side it remains
possible to photograph trains passing the still extant Selsdon station platforms. No 377155 heads towards South
Croydon in May 2008. *Both MHCB*

SELSDON: This view from the Elmers End line down platform at Selsdon shows East Grinstead-bound 3H DEMU No 1109 climbing the bank from South Croydon in 1972. The Oxted line had to put up with not very comfortable 3D and 3H diesel-electric units, certainly not a patch on the Bulleid steam stock they replaced, from the end of steam until the beginning of the 21st century. The 'present' view shows EMU No 377214 at the same location in May 2008.

A surprising number of seemingly innocent suburban stations have something of a story to tell and Selsdon is just such one. As a little lad I was puzzled by its name, for it seemed an awful long way from Selsdon itself. It had started out in 1885, honestly enough, as Selsdon Road. The Elmers End section was of typically South Eastern appearance, the

Oxted line part typically LB&SCR. In 1935, in a forlorn attempt to improve business, the Southern Railway renamed it Selsdon, which was a good 2 miles away. Unloved and neglected, it was the last station in London or its suburbs to feature gas lighting, a real anachronism seen against the 1950s and '60s high-rise flats and offices that caused Croydon citizens to dub their town 'Little Manhattan'. *Both MHCB*

RIDDLESDOWN is an Oxted line station on the outer fringes of suburbia, set deep in the slopes of the North Downs. In September 1955 former SE&CR 'H' Class 0-4-4T arrives with a stopping train from London Bridge to East Grinstead.

By May 2008 new lamp posts have appeared and a certain amount of modernisation has taken place, but the setting has changed little as DMU No 171727 heads through on its way to Oxted and Uckfield. *Both MHCB*

RIDDLESDOWN: 'C2X' No 32546 drifts down the bank through the station with a freight from Tunbridge Wells West in September 1955. These former LB&SCR 'C2' 0-6-0s dating from 1983-1902 were rebuilt with larger boilers and as such proved excellent engines, all still being in existence in 1955.

Electrification came to Oxted and East Grinstead, but not to Uckfield, in September 1987. Freight has long disappeared from the Oxted line. Southern DMU No 171804, on its way from Uckfield to London Bridge, emerges from Riddlesdown Tunnel in May 2008. *Both MHCB*

South, East and West Croydon

SOUTH CROYDON: Looking south in 1968, a six-coach train, with 2BIL No 2057 bringing up the rear, heads past the site of the disastrous accident of 1947 on its way to Brighton. Also in the picture are an RT bus and a typical Art Deco-style Southern Railway signal box.

At the same location in May 2008 are suburban EMU No 455829 on the left and First Capital Connect's No 319437 on the right. The signal box has gone, giving us a clearer view of the junction with the Oxted line. *Both MHCB*

SOUTH CROYDON: An eight-coach train of two 4LAVs, with No 2925 leading, speeds through South Croydon with a service from London Bridge to Reigate (the front section, which will be detached at Redhill) and Brighton.

In May 2006 First Capital Connect's No 319437 is on its way from Bedford to Brighton. The Class 319s led a revolution in London commuting habits. Until 1988 north was north and south was south and seldom would the twain meet outside the West End and the City. Only a suburban Londoner would understand the full implications of this. It was remarkable how those south of the Thames regarded the suburbs north of the Thames as alien, unexplored territory and vice versa. The Snow Hill line between Blackfriars and Farringdon, which had been almost exclusively used for freight, fell out of use in 1971. However, it gradually dawned upon a great many people that this could provide an enormously valuable passenger link between north and south, and so it has proved since an electrified service began in May 1988. Growth has increased every year and the system is planned to expand yet more. *Both MHCB*

SOUTH CROYDON: LB&SCR 'H1' Class 'Atlantic' No 38 passes South Croydon in about 1920 with an up Brighton express of distinctive 'balloon' stock incorporating a clerestory Pullman.

In April 2008 No 508203 is on its way from Victoria to Redhill and Tonbridge. The Class 508 EMUs were a development of the experimental PEPs, delivery beginning in 1979. Five years later they were sent to Merseyside, one of the trailers being removed and incorporated into new Class 455 units. In 1999 12 Class 508s returned to work on the South Eastern, being finally withdrawn at the end of 2008. *Pamlin/MHCB*

SOUTH CROYDON: LB&SCR 'E5' 0-6-2T No 591 approaches South Croydon with a Brighton express in about 1920. The LB&SCR was much addicted to the 0-6-2T wheel arrangement, using it for both freight and passenger locomotives. One of the mixed-traffic 'E4' 0-6-2Ts, *Birch Grove*, is preserved on the Bluebell Railway.

At the same location in April 1955 BR Standard 2-6-4T No 80012 heads a long rake of SE&CR-built non-corridor carriages bound for Tunbridge Wells West. The great majority of these excellent BR Standard tanks were built at Brighton and were the mainstay of Oxted line services until the end of steam.

Finally, at a location where rampant hedge growth has become obvious, a 'Gatwick Express' and a Southern Class 455 pass in May 2008. *Pamlin/MHCB (2)*

EAST CROYDON: A Stroudley 'single' (2-2-2) heads through East Croydon with an express for the Sussex coast in about 1890. East Croydon, one of Britain's busiest through stations, has a quite complicated history. Starting out as simply Croydon in July 1841, a second section, New Croydon, was opened when the line to Victoria was completed by the LB&SCR in 1860. Dog-in-the-manger-like, the Brighton line refused to let its partner at East Croydon, the South Eastern Railway, use it. Squabbles were a way of life between these two companies and it wasn't until the Southern Railway absorbed them both that the separate ledgers of takings kept by the two companies at East Croydon were amalgamated. By the end of the 19th century it had become a three-island-platform station, as now, with its present name.

Some 35 years later, in about 1925, a 'River' Class 2-6-4T speeds through with a down express. Hall and Co still has a prominent presence; the 'R1' 0-4-4T is standing on the track leading to that company's sidings, which are obscured by the train in the previous picture. The handsome 'River' Class was a Maunsell design, originating on the SE&CR, but very much in the Brighton line tradition of express tank engines. Unfortunately poor track maintenance on the Eastern Section led to a very bad accident at Sevenoaks in 1927 and the 'Rivers' were converted to 'U' Class 2-6-0s.

Finally, a 'Gatwick Express' eases its way through East Croydon in May 2008. *Pamlin/MHCB collection/MHCB*

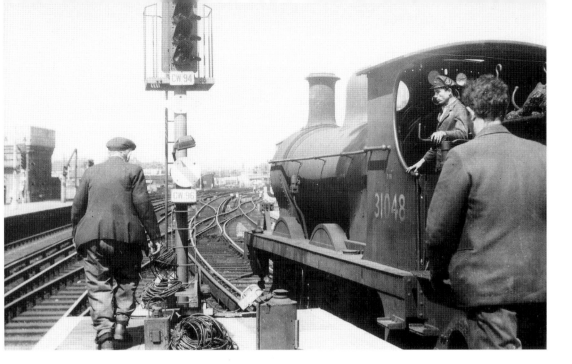

EAST CROYDON people: men at work on 13 May 1959, as '01' Class 0-6-0 No 31048 goes about its business as station pilot; a trilby-hatted businessman heads towards the station exit while 2BIL No 2093 departs from platform 3 in October, 1968; a passenger in May 2008; and a mother and son on the same platform in January 2007, while a 'Gatwick Express' Class 460 EMU passes platform 3. *All MHCB*

EAST CROYDON: These contrasting views of the exterior of the station date from about 1910 and February 2009, the latter featuring tram No 2546, newly repainted in blue, green and white livery, bound for New Addington. The light, airy new station, a vast improvement on the old, consisting of a large steel and glass frame suspended from a lightweight steel structure, was designed by Alan Brookes Associates, and built by YRM Anthony Hunt. It was completed in August 1992. *MHCB collection/MHCB*

89

EAST CROYDON: In this view looking back towards East Croydon station from the north in February 1969, a Class 33 diesel-electric locomotive has charge of inspection saloon No DS70155, converted from a Maunsell corridor carriage.

In January 2009 a 'Gatwick Express' passes through. Remarkably little seems to have changed in the immediate background in the intervening years, other than some paint on the terraced houses on the left and graffiti on the walls of their back gardens. *Both MHCB*

WEST CROYDON: In 1948 we see No S1810, one of the four two-car units converted when the West Croydon to Wimbledon line was electrified in 1929. They had originally been 1st Class carriages originally built for the LB&SCR South London overhead electric line in 1909. Unique in several respects, not least in that a gangway connected all compartments, they served a line that was single track for much of its length and surprisingly rural.

By 2008 track has been removed following Tramlink taking over the service between West Croydon and Wimbledon in May 2000. *Pamlin/MHCB*

Waddon, Epsom and Coulsdon

WADDON MARSH was the first station out of West Croydon on the Wimbledon line, photographed here in September 1968 with NOP EMU No 5662 about to depart. As can be seen, Waddon Marsh still boasted a signal box, semaphore signals and two platform faces at this time. After the demise of the original ex-LB&SCR units NOLs worked the branch for a while until being replaced, although in a sense the NOLs lived on for the NOPs were simply Bulleid bodies fitted on NOL underframes.

At the same location in May 2008, Tramlink car No 2542 heads for Wimbledon. *Both MHCB*

WADDON MARSH was situated in the heart of Croydon power station, the original gas works on both sides of the tracks and the post-war power station 'B' to the south across the A23 Brighton Road. In this picture, taken in the autumn of 1968, two of the locomotives used on the extensive internal railway system can be seen, a small electric one on the left, and an 0-4-0ST on the right.

At approximately the same location in May 2008, just about all that remains of the gas works is the gas holder seen on the extreme left of the picture. *Both MHCB*

WADDON MARSH: The Croydon by-pass, known as Purley Way, was opened in 1925 to relieve the heavy traffic in the town centre on the London to Brighton and Eastbourne roads, and passed beside the gas works and over the West Croydon to Wimbledon line at Waddon Marsh. In this picture taken from the Purley Way bridge in May 1969, a Class 33 is standing on one of the non-electrified tracks, having brought in a coal train to the power station, seen in the background, built on the Wimbledon side of Purley Way in 1950/1.

In May 2008 tram No 2552 passed the same spot heading for Croydon. *Both MHCB*

WADDON MARSH: A Peckett 0-4-0ST shunts at the power station in May 1969. Steam had disappeared from the British Rail network in the Croydon area some years before it finally gave way to diesel at the power station – the cab of a yellow-painted diesel shunter can be seen partly hidden by the building behind the Peckett.

The power station closed in 1984, was demolished in 1991, and in 1992 an IKEA store opened on the site. The two great chimneys were kept as a landmark, and the base of one can be seen in this May 2008 picture, while both of them can be seen in the one opposite. *Both MHCB*

MORDEN ROAD station is seen in 1950 with ex-LB&SCR '2' train No 1805.

If Morden Road gave the impression of being deep in the country some 60 years ago, things would seem to have grown even more rural today, with a Wimbledon-bound tram arriving. This is far from being an illusion, for the track runs alongside the extensive grounds of Morden Hall, now owned by the National Trust, and is complete with a river – the Wandle – a water wheel – which ground snuff into the 1920s – horses grazing and a rich selection of flora, a fair variety of mini beasts, the inevitable foxes, and some historic buildings. *MHCB collection/MHCB*

EPSOM DOWNS, opened by the LB&SCR in May 1865, had once been a very grand establishment of no fewer than nine platforms, visited regularly by royalty and tens of thousands of other race-goers. However, with the opening of the rival SER Tattenham Corner station, even nearer the racecourse, patronage began to decline and eventually, after a fire destroyed the signal box in 1982, it was reduced to this sad state, photographed in 1983, the entire branch from Sutton having been singled. Much of the land was sold off for up-market housing.

However, there has been a modest but welcome revival with a new station and, since being taken over by Southern, improved facilities, including automatic ticket machines and up-to-date train information. No 455833 has just arrived from Victoria in October 2008. *Both MHCB*

TATTENHAM CORNER: In August 1926 a former SE&CR 'H' Class 0-4-4T heads a train of six-wheelers. Beyond are some ex-LB&SCR and LSWR bogie carriages.

In May 2008 a Southern Class 456 has just arrived. This is not a station where passengers were ever encouraged to hang around on the often windy platforms. *H. C. Casserley/MHCB*

COULSDON NORTH: For a not very large town right at the very edge of suburbia, Coulsdon was liberally supplied with stations. This is Coulsdon North, where ex-LSWR torpedo-nose 4SUB No 4217 is taking a rest in March 1955 before heading back to Victoria. Coulsdon South was on the through route to the coast via Redhill, while Smitham, 100 or so yards from Coulsdon North, was on the Tattenham Corner line. Of rather more use would have been a station up the hill in the original village of Old Coulsdon, but residents had to make do with either the Central Area 59b bus or Country Area's 409/411. Coulsdon North, on opening in September 1899, rejoiced in the rather extraordinary title of Stoats Nest & Cane Hill, then, after a nasty accident in 1911, became Coulsdon & Smith Downs, in SR days assuming its final name.

In the second 'past' view, 'H2' No 32424 *Beachy Head*, destined to be the very last 'Atlantic' in ordinary service in the UK, is passing behind Coulsdon North with a London Bridge-bound trainload of Christmas parcels in December 1954. In those days a number of locomotives that had been in store from the beginning of autumn – not all of them veterans, as Bulleid 'Pacifics' fell into this category – emerged to haul the heavy Christmas traffic each year. As can be seen, a great variety of vans, some dating back to pre-Grouping days, also found employment. *Both MHCB*

COULSDON NORTH CARRIAGE SIDINGS can be seen at the top of the lower picture on the previous page. On 22 September 1929 the LB&SCR overhead electrics gave way to the third rail system, pioneered by the LSWR, and this picture of the Coulsdon North sidings, featuring on the left an overhead unit and on the right a third rail one, may well have been taken on that day.

Coulsdon North sidings in 1969 feature on the left a 6PAN express unit, a 4SUB proudly sporting its newly applied all-yellow nose, and a 4EPB. The 6PAN motor coach was by this date in departmental service, all the original SR express units having been replaced by BR-designed ones. *H. C. Casserley/MHCB*

COULSDON NORTH: A 'U1' Class 2-6-0 speeds past the long-disused through platforms on the Quarry Line in February 1955 with a rake of newly overhauled carriages from Lancing Works. In the background is Hall & Company's quarry, served by sidings, while the water column on the down platform is still occasionally needed to top up the steam-hauled freights that pass this way.

Coulsdon never really needed three stations. Business at the North one gradually declined and eventually in the autumn of 1983 it closed and was demolished, allowing track rearrangement in the area, particularly needed in order to accommodate the 'Gatwick Express' service. In early 1984 a coast-bound service of CIGs and BIGs can be seen in the distance heading down the main Quarry line past the derelict platforms and signal box shortly before demolition.

The A23 Coulsdon by-pass now occupies the site of what was Coulsdon North station. On the first Sunday in April 2008, a 'Gatwick Express' speeds southwards in a landscape transformed by a sudden, heavy snowfall. *All MHCB*

COULSDON SOUTH: Snow was far more common in southern England 50-odd years ago. An 'N' Class 2-6-0 heads along the down slow main line towards Coulsdon South in January 1955.

At the same location in June 2004 are a London-bound 4VEP in Connex livery on the up slow line and a Brighton-bound Thameslink Class 319 speeding down the fast Quarry line. The houses in the background have not changed, although trees and bushes are abundant where once there were none. *Both MHCB*

Former LB&SCR lines around Norwood Junction

SELHURST: The Selhurst Triangle is a complex series of lines and junctions between East and West Croydon, Norwood Junction and Selhurst stations. In this picture, taken in 1968, a 4EPB is on its way from Norwood Junction to West Croydon with a backdrop of high-rise office buildings, which sprang up in the late 1950s and '60s.

 In April 2008 a Southern Class 455 unit makes its way from Norwood Junction to Selhurst, passing over another 455 heading from East Croydon towards Norwood Junction. Yet more high-rise building have joined those of 40 years earlier. *Both MHCB*

SELHURST is also the location of a long-established depot. The first picture, from January 1969, shows the extensive freight sidings, with two Class 08 shunters in the foreground and a 12-coach CIG/BIG train passing along the Victoria-South Coast main line between Selhurst and East Croydon.

In 1979 a Class 33 is in charge of an empty stock train of BR Mark 1s, while in the sidings are withdrawn 4SUBs, including some 1925 Southern Railway examples converted to departmental service, and beyond a CIG/BIG express.

By May 2008 freight has quite vanished and Southern Class 377s appear to have a complete monopoly at Selhurst depot, apart from one Class 319. Over the years the 38-acre site has been extensively developed and upgraded, the latest project, completed in 2006, costing £115 million. Selhurst means 'dwelling in a wood', and there is still a surprising amount of greenery around the depot. *All MHCB*

SELHURST: Situated on the main LB&SCR line from East and West Croydon to Victoria, the arrival of the railway in the 1860s did much to boost the population of what had until then been a collection of cottages beneath the hills of Norwood, where the Crystal Palace was re-erected after the Great Exhibition of 1851. It is also the nearest station for Crystal Palace football ground. This picture was taken in about 1900, shortly before the line was quadrupled.

In April 2008 a Southern Class 377 departs from the up slow platform. *MHCB collection/MHCB*

SELHURST: The non-stop Victoria to Brighton 'Brighton Belle' approaches Selhurst shortly before its last run in April 1972. By this date the three five-car Pullman units had been repainted, to few people's liking, in BR blue and grey. The word 'Pullman' on the carriage sides disappeared, being replaced by 'Brighton Belle'. Although by then almost 40 years old, the units had no trouble keeping pace with the BR CIGs and BIGs, which worked the rest of the London to Brighton timetable, as I discovered on a cab trip. The cars were not even worn out, simply far too expensive to run with the large staff needed when all that most passengers required on the 55-minute run was a cup of tea or coffee.

A 'Gatwick Express' is seen at the same location in May 2008. Remarkably little of the surroundings would appear to have changed in the intervening 36 years. *Both MHCB*

NORWOOD JUNCTION: In 1969 Class 73 electro-diesel No 6035 is in the foreground, with five Class 33s in the sidings on the other side of the tracks. At this time there was heavy inter-regional freight traffic to and from Norwood yards.

By April 2008 freight locomotives have quite disappeared. A Southern Class 455 EMU shunts out of Selhurst depot, with Norwood Junction station in the distance. *Both MHCB*

NORWOOD JUNCTION loco shed was opened by the Southern Railway purely as a depot for goods and shunting engines. On view on 16 June 1961 are two 'W' 2-6-4Ts, 'K' and 'N' Class 2-6-0s, at least two 'C2X' 0-6-0s and a Class 08 diesel shunter. The four-track main line is on the extreme left, hidden by the coaling plant, and beyond that and on the extreme right are the up and down lines connecting Norwood Junction and Crystal Palace.

After the shed closed an engineers' depot took over the site. This is approximately the same view, but trees and bushes almost obscure it. The down Crystal Palace-Norwood Junction line curves in from the right. *Both MHCB*

CRYSTAL PALACE LOW LEVEL: In about 1920 an LB&SCR overhead electric train enters the station from the Norwood direction. Above the tunnel and beyond the trees can be made out part of the Crystal Place itself.

Viewed from a higher angle in 2008, a Southern Class 455 EMU leaves the tunnel. The track layout is the same, but the signal box has long gone, as has the immaculately attired station master. The tunnel and the trees above it remain, but beyond the trees there is nothing but parked cars, the Crystal Palace having burned down in 1936. *Pamlin/MHCB*

CRYSTAL PLACE LOW LEVEL: In 1977 a Norwood Junction-bound 4EPB is at the platform. The station was a remarkably extensive establishment with four platform faces, other disused or demolished ones and some impressive buildings, all of course on account of the Crystal Palace, the grounds of which adjoined the station. Re-erected on the Norwood Heights after the Great Exhibition of 1851, the Crystal Palace provided the railway with much business until its destruction in 1936 in one of the most spectacular fires that London has ever seen, wartime included.

A Class 455 unit is at the same location in March 2008. A rather delightful feature, just visible high above the train, directly over the passenger waiting to enter, is a glass pavilion forming part of the entrance and a reminder of the magnificent Crystal Palace itself. *Both MHCB*

THORNTON HEATH is the next station up the line from Selhurst. This is the frontage with a newly introduced Croydon Corporation tram, c1905.

By May 2008 the building has lost its tower, but where it used to sit can clearly be seen. The awning has gone but otherwise it appears largely unchanged – unlike the vehicles outside. *Contemporary commercial postcard/MHCB*

NORBURY: The very last run by the last 'Atlantic' active in ordinary passenger service on British Railways passes Norbury on 13 April 1958. No 32424 *Beachy Head* is hauling a replica Newhaven boat train, a speciality of the Brighton 'Atlantics' for many years. Highly efficient and always well-cared for in their long career – No 32424 was 47 years old – many regretted that this beautiful engine was scrapped; however, a replica, using a genuine GNR boiler upon which the LB&SCR design was based, is being built by the Bluebell Railway.

A Canadian-built General Motors Class 66/7 Co-Co, No 66717 of GBRF, owned by First Group, is at the same location approaching Norbury station with a ballast train in May 2008. Introduced by British Rail in 1999, at the latest count there are 579 of these 3,000bhp diesel-electric locomotives at work worldwide, and the class is still in production. *Both MHCB*

BROCKLEY: In August 1926 LB&SCR 'E1' Class 0-6-0T No B218 heads a train of six-wheel carriages. The 'E1s' were introduced by Stroudley in 1874 and proved immensely useful both as local passenger and goods engines, the last being getting on for 80 years old when withdrawn by British Railways. One has been preserved.

In the spring of 2008 a Class 456 unit takes the place of the 'E1' and its train. Three bridges still span the station, although all have been renewed since 1926. *H. C. Casserley/MHCB*

NEAR BROCKLEY: In about 1930 one of the magnificent LB&SCR 'Baltic' tanks, introduced in 1914, pounds up the bank between Brockley and Honor Oak Park with the most prestigious London Bridge to Brighton express of the day, the businessmen's 'City Limited', composed of recently introduced Maunsell corridors and one elderly clerestory-roofed Pullman.

Climbing towards Honor Oak Park in April 2008, Capital Connect No 319423 is on its way from Bedford to Brighton. The semaphore signals and the telegraph poles have long disappeared, but the long cutting remains a haven for flora and fauna. *O. J. Morris/MHCB*

To Victoria

WANDSWORTH COMMON: In 1994 a Class 20 passes on the up slow line with an engineers' train. These English Electric Bo-Bos were one of the most successful of the very early British Railways diesels, and although none were ever officially allocated to the Southern Region, they have been seen on various duties on Southern metals for the best part of 50 years.

In September 2008 Southern Class 377s occupy the down slow and up fast lines. There are a remarkable number of green oases alongside the Streatham Common to Battersea Park section of the line out of Victoria, and the area around Wandsworth Common is one of the most pleasant. *Both MHCB*

WANDSWORTH COMMON: In 1948 'I3' tank No 32027 is on the down fast line with an Oxted line train. These Marsh-designed 4-4-2Ts were one of the most successful tank engine designs of all time. Introduced in 1907, one of the tasks of the superheated examples was hauling the 'Sunny South Express' between Willesden Junction and Brighton, turn and turn about with LNWR 4-4-0s. The economy and efficiency with which they accomplished this gave Crewe something to think about and had a considerable influence on its subsequent designs.

The all-Pullman 'Brighton Belle', with unit No 3052 leading, running non-stop from Victoria to Brighton, passes Wandsworth Common in 1966.

Finally, a 'Gatwick Express' Class 460 passes in September 2008. Built by Alsthom, eight of these eight-car trains were introduced in 2001. Residential buildings now occupy the land immediately adjacent to the down slow platform, and the up fast platform, long disused, is now inaccessible, except to a lens poked through the railings. *MHCB collection/Colour-Rail/MHCB*

BATTERSEA PARK: In about 1950 an LB&SCR EMU dating from 1909, originally an overhead AC three-car unit but converted to a third-rail two-car one by the Southern Railway in 1928, arrives on a Victoria to London Bridge working.

The second picture shows the first of the 5701 Class of 2EPB units, shortly after introduction by British Railways in 1951. These replaced the original 1909 units.

The 2EPBs eventually gave way to the Class 456 units in 1991. No 456015 is seen in Network SouthEast livery in 1992, but they now wear Southern livery. *MHCB collection/ MHCB (2)*

GROSVENOR BRIDGE is used by trains from Battersea Park to cross the Thames and gain access to Victoria station. In this 1985 picture, on the right is one of the original 'Gatwick Express' trains, propelled by a Class 73, while on the left is a train comprising a 4EPB and a 2EPB unit of Bulleid design.

In July 2008 we see two Southern Class 377 units. The handsome Grosvenor Canal building of 1875 is partly obscured by trees, and beyond in both pictures is the Art Deco tower of Victoria Coach Station. *Both MHCB*

VICTORIA: The concourse of the LB&SCR section of the station is seen c1910. This achieved everlasting literary fame in *The Importance of Being Earnest* by Oscar Wilde, when Lady Bracknell, on being told that Ernest had been found as a newborn baby in a bag in the left luggage office of the Brighton line station, declaimed, 'The line is immaterial.'

On the Brighton side in January 2009, although much changed the roof is essentially as it was a century earlier. Opened in 1860 on land formerly occupied by the Grosvenor Canal, the London, Chatham & Dover and the London, Brighton & South Coast stations were two completely separate establishments, although 'joined at the hip', so to speak, and passengers had to go out into the street to get from one to the other. It was not until 1924 that the Southern Railway knocked a hole in the dividing wall and the two were united. In the early 1900s increasing business led the LB&SCR to extend its platforms so that two full-length trains could be accommodated in each, and could arrive and depart separately. In the 1980s a large shopping area, Victoria Place, was built over the Brighton line platforms, which no doubt generated a vast amount of revenue but rendered the platforms dark and gloomy. *London Transport Museum/MHCB*

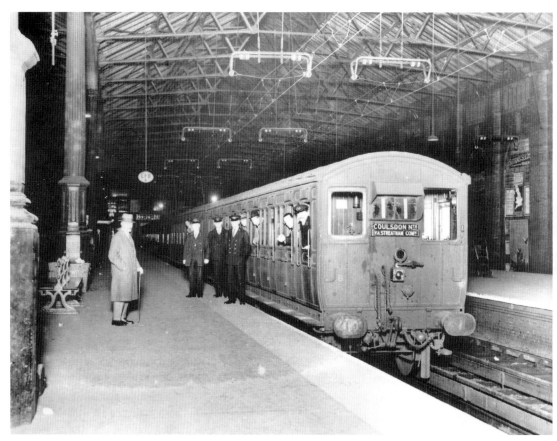

VICTORIA: Early on the morning of 23 September 1929 the last overhead electric is about to leave for Coulsdon North. Is this the ugliest front end of any electric train, ever?

At the end of 1956 BR's Southern Region, typically neither wanting nor wasting, re-formed 18 ancient LB&SCR wooden-bodied 4SUB units, Nos 4501-18, long past their sell-by date. No 4501, seen here on 22 May 1959, was unique in that two of its coaches, those nearest the barrier, were of LSWR origin.

During the 1980s rebuilding, the concourse was extended. A Southern Class 377 stands at approximately the same position, but further back, in December 2008. *H. C. Casserley/MHCB (2)*

Right Refilling the water tanks of the 'Brighton Belle', Victoria, 1971. *MHCB*

VICTORIA: LB&SCR Billinton 'B4' 4-4-0 No 52 is ready to depart from Victoria with a Brighton train, while in January 2009 a 'Gatwick Express' is at its own, dedicated and somewhat claustrophobic platform. *MHCB collection/MHCB*

VICTORIA: Passengers hurry out of the Brighton side of Victoria station in the late 1930s, contrasted with a rather more sedate scene in November 2008. The exterior of this side of Victoria is virtually unchanged, although 'bendy-buses' were unknown in the 1930s. *London Transport/MHCB*

VICTORIA: The most glamorous train to grace either side of Victoria station was the 'Golden Arrow', which conveyed passengers from the eastern side in Pullman splendour to Dover where they boarded a steamer for Calais and there took the French counterpart, the 'Fleche D'Or', to Paris. After being exhibited at the 1951 Festival of Britain exhibition on the South Bank of the Thames, BR Standard 'Britannia' Class 'Pacific' No 70004 *William Shakespeare* was sent to the Southern Region, together with No 70014, and kept in immaculate condition to work the 'Golden Arrow'. Here it is, complete with French and UK flags, in 1954.

Steam disappeared from boat trains in 1959 and Class 71 electric locomotives took over. This is the scene in 1972, shortly before the demise of the 'Golden Arrow'. By then it was a pale shadow of its former glorious self, the Pullmans reduced to just two or three vehicles, the rest ordinary BR Mark 1s. *Both MHCB*

VICTORIA: A porter loads the former Pullman car *Phoenix*, built just after the Second World War but now merely blue-and-grey-painted S302S, in 1972.

This, however, was not the end for *Phoenix*. Most appropriately, together with a selection of other Pullmans, it was bought and restored to its original chocolate and cream glory and put to work on the Venice Simplon Orient Express. It is seen here at Victoria in August 1991. *Both MHCB*

VICTORIA: Bulleid 4-6-2s were the usual motive power for the 'Golden Arrow' after its restoration following the war, and one of the 'light Pacifics' is seen here about to depart from Victoria in 1948.

Preserved steam can still be seen at Victoria from time to time. 'Battle of Britain' 'Pacific' No 34067 *Tangmere* is about to depart in May 2004. A Connex Class 455 can be seen at the far platform. *MHCB collection/MHCB*

STEWARTS LANE was the principal depot for steam services from both the Central and Eastern sides of Victoria. The as yet un-named 'Battle of Britain' 'Pacific' No 21C163, newly delivered from Brighton Works, poses at Stewarts Lane in 1947.

In 1990 an electro-diesel is seen. A 4CEP unit in 'jaffa cake' livery (the nickname given to the rather attractive but short-lived colour scheme on South Eastern long-distance EMUs) is passing on the viaduct in the background, heading for Victoria. *MHCB collection/MHCB*

INDEX OF LOCATIONS